A gift for:

From:

Coffee is Cheaper than Therapy

Ann Conklin Unruh

Ann Conklin Unruh

Illustrations by Kathleen Barnes

Cover Design by Elena Makansi
Cover Photo: Shutterstock

ISBN: 978-0-692-52471-8

Dedicated to three spritely spirits who enrich
their grandma's life:

Ellie

Jack

Bea

Acknowledgements

First, I want to thank my good friend Kathleen Wolfersberger whose conversation over coffee made this book possible.

My appreciation goes to Kathleen Barnes, the artist who created the coffee cup drawings.

Thank you friends for all of the interesting conversations and fun we have shared.

My good fortune is to have Sarah Grissom and Karen Sorensen-Unruh, two insightful daughters who have helped along the way with this book. Adam Grissom and Rissa Sorensen-Unruh, their spouses, simply make everything better.

Many thanks go to my editors from Blank Slate Communications, Kristina and Elena Makansi, for the cover design, formatting, and production of the book.

My gratitude goes to the readers, Kathy Baccarro, Vernida Carrier, Sarah Grissom, Annette Sorensen, and Eleanor Unruh for their ideas and observations.

Daily Bread is the restaurant where it all began. They provided pleasant service, tasty treats, and good coffee.

Saint Louis Publishers Association has been a good source of information.

Sometimes in life you just get lucky. That is what happened to me. I found a technical advisor, editor, and great guy all in one. Thank you, John.

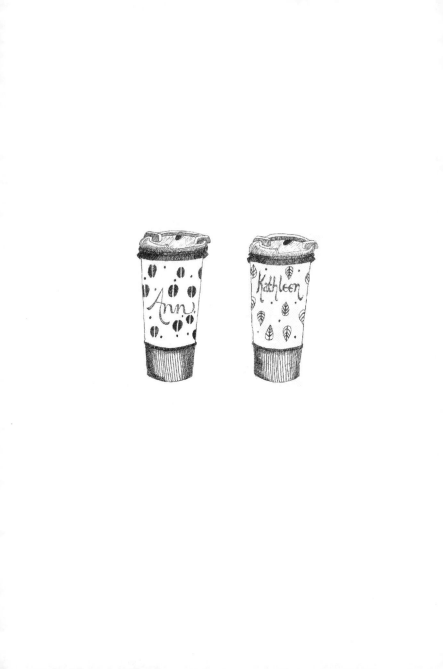

Introduction

It started out as two friends getting together over coffee. Kathleen and I would discuss the changing world and how we were changing. Often the ways that our friends, kids, grandchildren and even our moms dealt with life would come up. Many times the irony of it all would leave us laughing. All of this over coffee.

One day we went up to the counter for our usuals and the price had gone up twenty cents. That seemed like a rather steep jump. It caused us to observe that while the price had gone up "coffee was still cheaper than therapy."

So with the blessing of Kathleen, I am sharing some of the thoughts, frustrations and observations from these conversations. Grab a cup of coffee and listen in. I would love for you to join us.

Table of Contents

Percolating Ideas

Youth—What Happened?

. . . .

We were young for a long time. Now we are not so young. Occasionally, it still kind of shocks us.

A Good New Year's Resolution

. . . .

One morning over coffee Kathleen and I discussed New Year's resolutions. We resolved this year to embrace every compliment that comes our way. Don't resist it. Don't turn it back on the giver. But, take it to heart and enjoy it. Bring it out later to examine and enjoy some more.

Frankly, there are not enough compliments. We are going to savor each and every one. We'll receive them graciously and enthusiastically. This is going to be our new policy.

What to Do?

. . . .

Have you ever been in a conversation and had a really good thought that would definitely add to the discussion, but you didn't want to butt in and break up the flow? Then when it came time to speak, you had forgotten what you were going to say. The worst part was that you were the person speaking? How do you interrupt yourself?

St. Louis Cardinal T-Shirts

. . . .

Someone could make a great deal of money if they would sell Cardinal T-shirts that were flattering to women. Who designs these T-shirts? Surely not a woman. What we need is a greater selection of styles. The neckline definitely needs work. Perhaps something with a raglan sleeve which is both attractive and comfortable.

A classic blouse with a collar and front buttons would be nice. Add an insignia and you would be set. It could be worn anywhere. Not all women go to the games, but many would wear something nice looking to support the team. Especially, when we're winning!

The Downside of Decluttering

What would happen if closets were organized, drawers were sorted, kitchen cupboards were neat, the bathroom was straightened, the basement...ah the basement...was carefully set up in categories, papers were filed, and pictures were attractively arranged in albums? Would I become insufferable? Would I find it necessary to work into conversations how exceptional I was? Frankly, how could I help it?

Remember the Joy

. . . .

This message written by Anonymous was on a plaque at a combination gift shop/restaurant/gas station.

"Remember the Joy and not the Pain
Remember the Courage and not the Fear."

One of life's pleasures is to find wisdom in unexpected places. It is like coming upon a beautiful scene or running into an old friend.

Bra Straps, a Fashion Statement

. . . .

There is a fundamental difference between young and not-so-young women. It can be easily observed if you know what you are looking for. Get a group of young women together in the summer and there they are—visible bra straps. Colorful straps are popping their cheery selves out all over the place. You will see women wearing dramatic one shouldered tops and there on a bare shoulder is a brightly colored bra strap. You will see tank tops with cut away spots here and there and amongst it all will be colorful bra straps. It appears that the new rule is that bra straps can show, with one exception—they are very rarely white.

Now, get a group of more seasoned women together and very few bra straps will show. The ones that show will get discreetly tucked away, out of sight.

This is an interesting evolution. It would certainly be easier to dress if bra straps didn't need to be hidden. Not worrying about straps seems like a good idea but could a mature woman actually do it? Could she stand tall with straps showing clearly on the shoulder? Hmmm....

Book Titles That Say It All

. . . .

There are book titles that are so marvelously descriptive that it's not necessary to read the book. What a gift of time saved! They convey the message so well that you can absorb it easily and move on.

A few examples are:

Everybody's Normal Till You Get to Know Them

14,000 Things to be Happy About

I'm Okay, You're Okay

Everything I Need to Know I Learned in Kindergarten

I'll Mature When I'm Dead

Everyone Poops

Eye Openers

A Grown Up Moment

. . . .

When insulted, treated unfairly, or someone is needlessly rude, it is possible to have a grown up moment. This is when you can step back and say to yourself, "That was just plain wrong, but life happens, and I can move on."

When it is possible not to react to someone else's negative behavior, it is absolutely liberating. The ability to be an adult, to deal with churlish behavior, stupid thinking and not be dragged down by it, puts one at the top of the maturity pyramid. And life is good at the top!

To Color or Not to Color?

. . . .

Many women look very attractive with white hair. It enhances their essence and style. Other women choose never to have white hair. My mother colored her hair until she was 95. How could I not color? It would make my mother look bad.

Family Visits

. . . .

It is a joy to see the family when they come to town. They brighten up the world. The challenge is finding the right mix of activities that are fun for everyone, especially if you have more than one generation. Add to that the weather that is often too hot or cold and it's a challenge.

The Wee Ones, They Can Challenge You

. . . .

There is a little girl who is three and cute as a button. She has decided that she will make all of the decisions about her life. For instance, she does not wish to wear socks and shoes. You may have known a little one like this. You just have to love them and let the parents deal with the rest.

Seeing the Best
in Ourselves

. . . .

Positive feedback is exhilarating, thought provoking, and empowering. It brings out the best in a person. When you are around people who see the best in you, something happens— you walk a little taller, suck your stomach in a little more (at least metaphorically), and go forward with more confidence. Mark Twain once wrote that he could live on a good compliment for six months.

John's mother said, "I bake pies because people tell me how good they taste." She always received compliments, many times, from many different people. It would be hard to eat a piece of her pie without being moved to compliment her.

An acquaintance, who has been through several layoffs, said he looked for a job four days a week, and he spent the fifth day volunteering. He said, "They love you when you volunteer." It balanced him out. It was planned affirmation. He was working on the same principle as John's mother.

It may seem a bit contrived, but surrounding yourself with people who see the best in you is a wise decision. It is like holding up a mirror that allows you to see the best in yourself.

Stages of Life

. . . .

First you are young, then comes middle age. What do you call the stage after that? Most names seem distasteful, old, elderly, senior citizen etc. Recently a friend read a book that described this stage as "ageless," while not ideal, it seems to be the best so far.

Don't Forget Your Sweater

. . . .

Why is it that when the weather warms up, many restaurants cool down? This means having to carry a sweater. It can be 95 degrees out, and it's "sweater weather" inside. While restaurants are the most irritating, it happens in grocery stores, movie theaters, malls, and even churches. This makes no sense in a world that is trying to save energy.

When Trouble Strikes, Talk to a Friend

. . . .

When a health problem strikes it might be something you have never heard of before. Then suddenly, it'll be on the news. You'll find any number of people who have had it or know someone close to them who has. These people can be valuable resources. They can be as informative as your doctor, providing practical helpful information.

Louise had plantar fasciitis (a really strange name). A woman she just met told her that she had the exact same thing, and had gone to an acupuncturist, who made her better. When Louise went to that acupuncturist, she got better too. She never would have considered this before meeting the woman. Now she recommends acupuncture to others. Knowing someone has experienced the same problem and come out the other side is a comfort. It is helpful to know your situation is not unique and you are not alone.

Age Without Numbers

. . . .

Marge a lawyer, architect, first grade teacher and friend, thinks we should stop keeping track of our age by numbers. In fact, she thinks we should just stop thinking about age. Who hasn't had at least a moment of sadness or perhaps sheer terror at the thought of entering the next decade? Consider this: if the numbers went away, there wouldn't be a next decade. If there were no numbers, we wouldn't have to worry about ageism or being too young to be taken seriously.

Sometimes numbers don't matter at all, but sometimes they can weigh you down. If they went away we might have a more comfortable existence. It would be hard to accomplish, but if it happened it could be liberating. Think of the possibilities.

Good Mental Health, Everybody Needs It

. . . .

A great deal is written about taking care of your physical health. Not nearly as much is written about taking care of your mental health. But as most everyone knows, when that goes bad, it casts a huge shadow. To say the very least, it weighs one down.

Here are seven ideas for maintaining mental health to consider:

Keep positive people in your life. Their perspective can rub off.

Say something flattering and generous to someone. With luck, if you pay a good compliment, it could make their day, or at least the next 15 minutes.

Stand up straight and smile. It is good for what ails you.

Fake it. Act like you are a well-balanced, upbeat, healthy person.

Moisturize!

Exercise. Get your endorphins firing.

Get a haircut. A good haircut can do wonders.

Free at Last

. . . .

"Do the best you can and move on." Let's change that to "Do a reasonably good job and move on." The idea that you don't have to try your best at everything is liberating.

What's Brewing

Yes!

. . . .

"Life isn't about waiting for the storm to pass;
it's about learning to dance in the rain."

~ Vivian Greene

Class Reunions

Blessings to all of the class members on the reunion committee! You do a great service for the class. One small request: when you make the name tags, would you print the first name in HUGE letters? There are some in the class who would be very appreciative.

Things to Think, But Not to Say

. . . .

These are statements to avoid, even though they slip out so easily and do really make the point:

"Wish they would turn the lights up so I could see the menu."

"My first job paid…"

"People aren't loyal to their employers like they used to be."

"Back in the day…"

"I remember when candy bars only cost ten cents."

"You'd think in church they could dress a little better."

"My car costs more than my first house."

"Do they have to play that music so loud?"

"I can't believe how these young people act."

"That doctor looks like he is about 14."

Flab vs Youth

. . . .

Here is how it happened: a little girl I know pointed out that there was extra skin hanging from my underarm. She had very little, her mother had some, and I had the most. She didn't call it skin, she called it "flab." I renamed it for her.

So putting a positive spin on it, I said, "If she was lucky when she got older, she might have some extra skin, too. It's good to have extra skin!"

Then bless her little heart, she kind of got into it. We started thinking up the virtues of extra skin. She thought of ways it might be handy, if you needed some extra skin, it would be stored right there. My contribution was that it could be considered a sign of beauty. It really is all about your perspective.

Is It Morbid to Talk About Mortality?

. . . .

Death, in general, seems to be a taboo subject. It could be healthy to discuss it, but it often feels uncomfortable. We can talk about ailments, sometimes at great length, but death is different. We might be in a better position to deal with death, ours and those near to us, if we talked about it with our friends. Other perspectives could be helpful in getting comfortable with the idea. There is the possibility, that if you talked more about death, it could impact how you lead your life.

Folk Wisdom

. . . .

Some of these fit, sometimes:

- Life is like a good wine; it improves with age.
- It sure beats the alternative.
- Your age is catching up to you.
- A senior moment.
- From the back of a galloping horse, it is good enough.
- With age comes wisdom.

Values

·····················

When people start talking about their values, they are often implying that their values are better than other people's. Sometimes I am one of those other people.

Nothing Goes

. . . .

It's the strangest thing. When getting ready for a trip, all of a sudden nothing in my wardrobe goes together. During the rest of the year, my clothes more or less cooperate, but pull out the suitcases and there's trouble. It doesn't make a lot of sense. Does this happen to other people?

Time to Say Goodbye

. . . .

Well worn bras are wonderful. They're soft. They're comfortable. What's not to love? Each and every one is dear. But there comes a time when they must be replaced. Oh, the chagrin one can feel when walking through Macy's and catching a side glimpse of oneself in a long mirror. Goodness, the time has come! You know what that means. There is the process of figuring out the right size. Whatever the size, there will be relatively few bras to choose from. It is a strange thing and always the same -- not as many choices as desired. Next there is the issue of cost. Bra shopping can give severe sticker shock.

It takes a while to build up the courage for this adventure. Maybe something new has come along. Rumor has it there are amazing things going on in the world of lingerie. Many of them are uplifting!

How Many Wardrobes?

. . . .

A closet has many wardrobes. First, there are the clothes currently being worn. Second, there are clothes that are too small, but any day now they might fit. And then, there are the clothes that are too large. While I don't want it to happen, I might grow into them. It costs a lot of time and money to replace these unworn wardrobes, so it may be best to hold onto them, just in case.

The discouraging part is to have all of these clothes, but nothing to wear tonight!

Black is Nice, But...

. . . .

It is so easy to buy black. There's lots of it in the stores. It can be worn year-round. While clothes generally come in several colors and black, the colors are often not quite right. But if the style is flattering and it fits, another black item goes into the wardrobe.

Black can be sophisticated or somber. Next to the face, sometimes, it can drag one's features down. Colors on the other hand can give you a lift. Looking at someone in an attractive flattering color can be cheering and can send a positive vibe. I am challenging myself to buy color.

Refill and Refresh

Flats

. . . .

Recently, during lunch, a friend pointed out that the bottom of her feet were hurting. She was really disturbed because she thought it meant she was getting old. Would she be reduced, she wondered, to wearing rubber-soled flats? There sitting across from her, under the table were my rubber-soled flats. (I like to think they allow me to be more agile.)

Her feet must have improved because the next lunch I had with her she was back in stylish high heels. And yes, I was in rubber-soled flats. Neither of us brought up the subject of shoes.

Help, I Can't Get Out of the House

. . . .

Why does it take so long to get out of the house? Getting collected, presentable and out the door is not something to take lightly. Heaven help if keys or purse are lost. This is quite annoying. Now, there is a new twist, a restroom stop before leaving.

Is it genetic? Is it age? Is it gender? For some reason, it doesn't seem to happen as much to men.

Keeping the House

. . . .

Many times when I was with Mother, one or another of her friends would say, "All I really care about is being able to keep the house." I would think to myself, "What you really need to do is get out of that house!" It seemed very clear that they could use their time and energy having fun, getting together with friends, and generally enjoying themselves. Instead they were spending their time and money trying to keep their house up.

Now I am developing an appreciation for their thinking. This, must be irony. The house has become my home. It didn't start out that way. It just seemed like the place I lived. I remember when we moved in, looking at the backyard and thinking, "Let's blacktop the whole thing. When we want to look at plants, we'll go to the Botanical Garden." Now the backyard has become my little botanical garden. When did this happen? What other ironies does life have in store?

Sometimes Better,
Sometimes Worse

. . . .

There is a certain irony to the fact that as one matures, self-esteem still requires work. The reality seems to be, that as life goes on, self-esteem ebbs and flows. We are largely responsible for our own self-esteem, whether that is a burden or a comfort is hard to say. Sometimes it is a little of each.

It's Not Obvious

. . . .

Health problems become more common as the years advance. Almost everyone has some kind of issue. Not everyone talks about them, but if you scratch the surface, there they are. Many people look healthy, seem to be fit, and appear to be in a really good place. One would never guess that they have any health issues. You find out that they do, in interesting ways. Sometimes it comes up in conversation. Doctor's appointments start to interfere with plans. Parking close, so it is not too far to walk, has more significance.

Did you ever think you or your friends would have ailments? It might be normal but they still come as a surprise.

Tight Pants

. . . .

What do you do when your pants are too tight? It is a dilemma. Do you swallow your pride and go to larger pants? Do you stuff yourself in those too tight pants and suffer? When taking the suffer route, one wonders: "How long can I make it? Will I cave?"

Enough of This, Already!

. . . .

Here is what happened: I was at the mall and it suddenly started to rain. While waiting at the door for the rain to let up, a nice looking, middle-aged man came up and looked out. We commented on the weather. He mentioned the weather in Utah where he was from. I mentioned the weather on a recent trip. Next he asked if the mall had a particular store. "Not that I was aware of," I responded. Then I added, " I walk here most every day."

Next, get this: he said, "MY MOTHER WALKS AT THE MALL, TOO." On and on he went, describing the virtues of mall walking — you get to see people, it's good exercise, it get's you out of the house etc. etc. I can't remember the rest of what he said because …well it was just too much!

Is it Dinner Time Again?

. . . .

What is it about grocery shopping, planning meals, and fixing food? For some of us, the longer we live, the less inclined we are to want to do this. Is it because we are responsible for feeding fewer people? Did we never want to fix food but really didn't have a choice?

As we cook less, we forget what the good meals were we prepared in the past. So, it becomes harder to come up with ideas when you are inclined to cook. Perhaps it is because there are more options for eating out, although dining out is not always that appealing. Everyone eats. It would be interesting to know what they are eating and who is preparing their meals.

What Is Going On
With Cucumbers?

. . . .

Have you noticed that when you cut into a cucumber there are an enormous number of seeds? What's going on? Are they feeling tremendous pressure to reproduce? Sometimes it seems like 2/3 of a cucumber is seeds. It hasn't always been this way. Has it? It's gotten to the point where it is necessary to deseed them, before putting them in a salad. It takes more time, and they don't look as good. It's aggravating.

How Are You, Really?

. . . .

This question takes on more meaning as we grow older. It used to be that the common answer was "Fine." Not so much anymore. As always, the first question that comes to mind is, do they really want to know how you are or is it just conversation? The second question is, do you really want to tell them?

More people seem to be sharing how they are. Good or bad, it feels better when someone gives an honest take on themselves or their situation. Often a few authentic words can create a more meaningful connection than a lot of superficial conversation.

Bottomless Cup

Two Ways to Go

. . . .

People age in two ways. The first way is a gradual process. Slowly, over time, a person grows older looking. The second way is more dramatic. An individual goes along looking the same for quite a long time, then suddenly aging happens in a spurt. It is possible for a person to age first one way and then the other.

The first way of aging, slow and steady, is what it is. There is not too much to say about it. The second way, holding and then going down fast can be gratifying for a while. When others are slipping, you are holding. But when you fall into the aging abyss, it can be quite discouraging.

One lesson to take from this is, if you are in a holding pattern, it's a good time to have your picture taken.

The Christmas Question

. . . .

When someone asks, "Are you ready for Christmas?" there's one sure thing. They are! It seems like they pick out people who might be running a bit behind and pose this question. If you are one of the askers, have a heart and phrase your question a little more gently. Remember the Christmas spirit.

Weddings and Funerals

. . . .

The first part of life is all about weddings, while they continue throughout life, gradually funerals begin to occur more often.

Weddings and funerals do have a great deal in common. They are often in a church. They have music, sometimes with a soloist singing lovely songs. There is a program and a fairly consistent format. Family members and friends sometimes do readings. The clergy make thoughtful remarks.

Now, not only are weddings called "celebrations," so are funerals. Afterwards, there is a time to greet people and have refreshments. It seems a bit ironic, but perhaps it is not. These are both tremendously significant events in a life. One is a ceremony to mark a beginning and the other marks an ending.

Do You Read the Obituaries?

....

Do you check to see what age the person was when they died and what caused their death? These things would be interesting to know. Sometimes obituaries have youthful pictures of very old people. Did the deceased want that? Some people write their own. What will be said in my obituary? It would be interesting to know.

Pot Holes

. . . .

Pot holes might be considered a metaphor for the challenges in life.

Increasingly pot holes represent holes in the pavement that rattle your bones and mess with your car's alignment. It is getting serious when you start picking the streets for the drive home based on the number of pot holes you will encounter. Recently a news show featured pot holes that had been filled with dirt and had flowers blooming in them. If the street department can't fill the holes it would be helpful if they painted bright colors around the rims. It would make it easier to drive. Even when you know they are there, those devils can sneak up on you.

Not So Nice

. . . .

Not everyone wants to talk with older people. They simply ignore them. When this happens a rewarding experience can be missed. What a shame.

Toastmasters

. . . .

At a January meeting of Toastmasters, a member stood up and gave the Thought for the Day. Here is what he said: "Don't carry last year's baggage into this year. Leave it behind." It was quiet in the room when he finished speaking. You could almost hear people thinking.

Albuquerque, New Mexico and Norfolk, Virginia

. . . .

These two cities may seem diverse but they have one thing in common. They have great airports. The words "great" and "airport" don't normally go together. However, in this case they do.

The Albuquerque Airport is charming. It has loads of colorful New Mexican art, a variety of gift shops filled with interesting items, and a waiting area with a generous number of chairs. At Christmas time you may find choirs singing, and groups playing musical instruments to welcome soldiers and travelers home for the holidays. This is a fun place.

The Norfolk, Virginia Airport is also charming but in a different way. As you approach it is like driving into a lovely tree filled park. It's quite amazing. The Airport itself has huge floor to ceiling windows, when you step inside it feels like you are still outside in the park. Adding to this impression are the many green plants and trees placed through out the building. You come away with a feeling of peace and tranquility. Not what you would expect from an airport.

What a Deal!

. . . .

What a bargain! These are words to live for. Now 50% off is very good. You can't complain about that. But the real fun begins when you hit 75% and if you get very lucky you might find something at 80% off. Oh, it makes the heart sing and puts a smile on your face if you are a dedicated shopper. For an adrenalin rush, it's hard to beat a good sale!

Responsible

. . . .

Is it always good to be responsible? Do you know someone who is so good at being responsible that everything gets dumped on them? Is it you? We know some folks with this problem and it doesn't seem fair. These are some ideas that might help one get out of this bind:

> Smile and say, "I don't know how."
>
> Leave a mess now and then.
>
> Postpone returning some calls.
>
> Leave minor tasks undone.
>
> Quote eccentric, unconventional people.
>
> Be unpredictable.
>
> Talk about forgetting to pay a bill on time.

One Cup at a Time

Who's in Charge?

. . . .

Have you ever met someone who said something that made you think, "We must have had the same mother!" A friend said, "My mother could not get rid of anything unless she knew it was going to a good home." Boy, do I understand that!

There must be a thousand unstated or stated rules that came from Mother. They have shaped me. Some are so ingrained that I really don't notice them. Some I have made a conscious effort to lose. Some I treasure.

Mother would come to visit. If there were 12 peas left over, she would say, "Don't throw those away; I'll eat them." Recently, I went to visit my nephew. There were 11 really nice green beans left, and I said, "Don't throw those away! We can eat them later." Then I kicked myself. Where did that voice come from? Surely not me! I think Mother took possession of my body. Then again, maybe she has been there all the time.

Is this Zen?

. . . .

When you are really young, multi-tasking is hard. With age and practice, it gets easier. Then somewhere along the way it seems to get harder again. But here is the interesting part: it also becomes less appealing. There is a certain satisfaction in focusing on doing one thing at a time. Is this Zen? It would be nice to think so.

Happy Holidays

. . . .

Some years holidays are very enjoyable. It's fun to celebrate the traditions and everything that goes with them. Other years the spark isn't there. It becomes more of an effort to get in the spirit. A number of friends have made this observation. So what can one do when this happens? Perhaps just ride along on other's enthusiasm and enjoy the holiday as much as possible.

It's Back

. . . .

The girdle has returned, but now it's called "Spanx." They are pretty much the same. It appears we have come full circle. Well, not for all of us. Some prefer to be comfortable in their own skin, without the benefit of a second skin. Other women opt for the trimmer look. Either way it is nice to have a choice.

No More Tiny Little Numbers

. . . .

What is going on with price tags? Have you noticed that on some items, particularly women's clothes, numbers on the tag are incredibly small. So small that even with glasses you have to squint to see how much it costs? What could be the reasoning behind this? Sometimes I have to track down a young clerk to read it. You would think that the size of the price would be larger to make it easier for the customer to read. Lately, not only is it hard to read, but it is difficult to find where the price is located on the tag. Help us out retailers.

Hot Weather Favorites

· ·

Sandals

Sun hats

Outdoor concerts

Beach

Walking in the park

Outdoor dining

Vera's Bourbon Slush

Vera's Bourbon Slush

. . . .

Stir together the following ingredients:

2 cups strong tea
1 ¼ cups sugar
12 oz. can frozen orange juice
 concentrate, thawed
12 oz. can frozen lemonade, thawed
2 cups bourbon (Canadian Mist
 Whiskey is very good)
7 cups water

Place in freezer at least 24 hours before serving. (Vera likes to stir it several times while it is freezing.) Then stir it just before serving. Sometimes served with a spoon.

Salud!

Cold Weather Favorites

. . . .

Fires in the fireplace

A good book

Winter Olympics

Cuddle Duds

Knee socks

Cuties

Boots

Kathleen's Hot Toddy

Kathleen's Hot Toddy

· ·

In a glass coffee mug add:

> 1 tablespoon of sugar
> (real maple syrup can be substituted).
> Dissolve it with a little hot water.
>
> 1 twist of lemon peel (bruise firmly)
> 4 cloves
> 1 stick of cinnamon
> 1 generous jigger (1 ½ oz.) of bourbon

Fill the rest of the mug with steaming hot water. Stir gently.

Enjoy!

Maintenance

. . . .

Personally, it seems as though entirely too much time is spent performing routine maintenance chores. Yet in the same breath there is more that could be done. The house is in constant need. It's best when the house looks good. But often it feels that too much of life is spent tidying, organizing, and cleaning. It would be nice to revolt but it is not quite clear how that would work.

The world seems to have a high standard of neatness. This is probably why people like to get together at restaurants. It's just easier than making sure the bathroom is clean and the house is neat.

Winter Weight

. . . .

What is it about winter that makes you want to eat? Let's not talk about salads. In fact, salads no longer are of interest. Beef stew followed by apple pie, then later on in the evening a little snack or two. It's like being a bear, and needing to build up fat for the winter. There is no point asking yourself, "Why do I want to eat? Am I bored? Am I lonely? Am I unhappy?" Who knows? Who cares? Just bring on the food!

Oh No, Not January

· ·

Are the circles under one's eyes darker in January? Does most of the year's aging happen in January? Is this correlated to the fact that the coldest day of the year is in January? Is there any hope in January? Perhaps the best piece of advice comes from a friend who advises, "Just keep going and don't think too much."

(Written in January.)

Good to the Last Drop!

Who Gets the China?

The china is rarely used. Even on very nice occasions, it will often get passed over. It is lovely but not particularly convenient. Will it ever be back in style? Will there be a time when every bride will want it? When my generation goes, where will the china go?

A New Place

. . . .

There are advantages to living in a condo or a planned a community. Someone else shovels the snow. If they are slow about it, you can complain. It is much easier to complain than to shovel snow. When you go on a trip, someone else is already watering the lawn and tending the plants. You don't have to pay extra money or feel indebted. If you are lucky, there will be pleasant neighbors to chat with, and you won't have to go out in the cold or heat to see them. Expenses are more predictable.

This could be good. It is something to consider.

Something to Consider

. . . .

The ideal condominium or planned community would have:

- a living room large enough to have friends over
- a balcony or patio that would allow one to step outside
- one floor
- a full-sized washer and dryer in the unit
- space to have the children and guests stay when they come to visit
- a price substantially less than the selling price of your house
- a good location

- modest fees and
- a good mix of older and younger people.

So far the ideal remains elusive. It is interesting to listen to friends as they explore housing options. One couple found their ideal community in Florida.

First You're Busy
Then You're Not

. . . .

What is it about life? Sometimes one is really busy, working hard to get everything done, running fast just to stay in place. Then, when there is more free time, that's when you think, "Now what was I going to do when I had some time?" and nothing comes to mind, or at least nothing one is interested in doing. Maybe the thing to do, while you are very busy, is to make a list of all the things you would like to do, but don't have the time for at the moment.

A Compliment?

. . . .

Recently overheard in our local coffee shop, "You are looking well-preserved!" Was this some weird form of compliment or perhaps the ultimate insult?

It Finally Happened

Today it happened. I bought a matronly looking swimsuit. I tried on suits with ruffles, over-blouses, swirls of material across the front, on and on. I don't understand it. I have been bigger in the past, but somehow the suits I was trying on seemed to make me look worse. Then I tried on a suit only a grandmother would wear and decided to go with it. It was a sobering moment.

I must admit the suit was comfortable. The neckline showed no cleavage. The back was relatively high so it covered up, as they say, "a multitude of sins." I didn't have to arrange the pant line because you can't see the pants with the skirt. Sounds grim, doesn't it? But after five or so minutes of trauma, I accepted it. My mind immediately began to rationalize. Maybe my body isn't so hip. I just put some really trendy pillows on my couch. My couch is hip. That ought to count for something. And now several hours later, as I think back over my swimsuit experience, I'm okay with it. This is rather shocking to me. I seem to be moving on. You don't suppose that this is a sign of maturity, do you? Somehow it doesn't seem worth my time to sulk about it. I have better things to do, bigger fish to fry. I have to admit I am almost pleased with myself. Can you believe this? It's hard for me to believe.

The Beach

. . . .

1st day—Put on swimsuit. Observe waistline. Be strong. Carry on.

2nd day—Observe humanity. What a marvelous array of shapes, sizes, colors and ages.

3rd day—Find my groove. Notice all of the interesting ways people experience the beach.

4th day—Put on swimsuit. Observe with new perspective. Consider getting a new suit. Maybe a two piece.

Zest vs Cynicism

. . . .

"I don't want to get bitter as I grow older," said a wise man in his 70s. It is easy to become a little jaded or a little cynical as one journeys through life.

But the zest! We can't lose the zest for life, the twinkle in the eye, the ability to laugh out loud or to get tickled over something. Don't you love when you meet someone who is just fun to be around? A positive outlook is a wonderful thing. It is so worth nurturing, if for no one else other than yourself.

The Pleasure of Being a Great-Aunt

. . . .

Life has extra bonuses. When we were young and contemplated life, we never gave any consideration to the pleasure of being an aunt, certainly not being a great-aunt. It is, well—it's great! Little is required. Parents do the work. If there is any work left over, grandparents take care of it. There is nothing left for a great-aunt to do, but simply enjoy. As these young folks progress through life, in addition to enjoying them, and being proud of their accomplishments, it's possible to take some credit. There's no denying sharing some family DNA. If you choose, historical touches and depth can be added to a conversation. After all, who is going to refute you, when you say, "His grandfather did the same thing".

Another pleasure comes in having such a title. Most titles require some work. Being a doctor or president certainly does, but for a great-aunt, there is no membership fee and no continuing education credits. Being a great-aunt is rather like being queen. It is simply yours forever!

First Words

. . . .

There is something so delightful about a child's first word. When will it come? What will it be? You wait. You wonder. Some first words are predictable, others seem to come right out of the blue. One dear little boy's first word was "banana." Clear and distinct "banana." His parents got busy and bought loads of bananas. It turned out he didn't like bananas. He just liked to say the word. In fact he referred to everything as "banana." Where did that come from? Nature, nurture? You wonder?

Gotta Love this Gal's Thinking!

. . . .

Recently at a 50th wedding anniversary party, a friend leaving the dance floor groaned, "My feet are killing me!" Looking down at her feet, I commented, "Cute shoes!" She said, "I wear them so that people don't look at my neck!" There are some great women, in this world, who keep it all together and carry on with spirit. You gotta love them!

Treasures

．．．．．．．．．．．．．．．．．．．．．．

One of life's pleasures is meeting an old friend whom you haven't seen in years and picking up the conversation as though you have never been apart. You can jump from the past to the present. You are on the same wave length again. When this happens it is an experience to be treasured.

Discussion Questions

. . . .

1.   If you were to choose three words to live by what would they be?

2.   Is there anything you are doing now that you never thought you would?

3.   Do you mind if I ask your age?

4.   How do you add a little interest to your life when you are bored?

5.   If you were to "just get by," what would be necessary for you to have or do?

6.   Do you attend class reunions? What surprised you?

7.   What are the minefields in life that seem to bring you down?

8. What do you think about when considering moving from your present home?

9. Who are some of your oldest friends with whom you stay in touch?. What do you like about them?

10. Give three questions to ask a younger person, that will get them talking to you.

11. What is your favorite coffee cup? Where did you get it? Tell us about it.

12. Do you have a favorite coffee shop? What do you like about it?

About Ann

Ann Unruh has an MA in counseling. She has been a teacher and a counselor. She lives in Kirkwood, Missouri with her husband John. She has two great kids and three adorable grandchildren.

Made in the USA
San Bernardino, CA
27 September 2015